Brands We Know

Disney

By Sara Green

Bellwether Media • Minneapolis, MN

Jump into the cockpit and take flight with Pilot books. Your journey will take you on high-energy adventures as you learn about all that is wild, weird, fascinating, and fun!

This edition first published in 2015 by Bellwether Media, Inc.

No part of this publication may be reproduced in whole or in part without written permission of the publisher.
For information regarding permission, write to Bellwether Media, Inc.,
Attention: Permissions Department,
5357 Penn Avenue South, Minneapolis, MN 55419.

Library of Congress Cataloging-in-Publication Data

Green, Sara, 1964-
 Disney / by Sara Green.
   pages cm. -- (Pilot: Brands We Know)
 Includes bibliographical references and index.
 Summary: "Engaging images accompany information about The Walt
Disney Company. The combination of high-interest subject matter and
narrative text is intended for students in grades 3 through 7"-- Provided
by publisher.
 Audience: Ages 7-12.
 Audience: Grades 3-7.
 ISBN 978-1-62617-205-0 (hardcover : alk. paper)
1. Walt Disney Company--History--Juvenile literature. 2. Disney, Walt,
1901-1966--Juvenile literature. I. Title.
 PN1999.W27G64 2015
 384'.80979494--dc23
                        2014041336

Printed in the United States of America, North Mankato, MN.

Table of Contents

What Is Disney?

Watching movies together is a fun activity for many families. Disney movies often top the list of family favorites. They have been entertaining people since the 1920s. Mickey Mouse was Disney's first famous character. Over the years, people have fallen in love with Snow White, Bambi, and many other Disney friends. More recently, Elsa, Anna, and Olaf from *Frozen* have become audience favorites.

Mickey Mouse

The Walt Disney Company, also known as Disney, is one of the largest entertainment businesses on Earth. It is worth about $143 billion. Disney **headquarters** are in Burbank, California. The company owns film and television studios. It publishes books and records music. It also runs several theme parks and a cruise line. Many people grow up watching Disney movies or using Disney products. They trust the **brand** from their childhood. In 2014, this led Disney to be named the most **reputable** company in the world!

By the Numbers

about
166,000
employees in
40
countries

32
Academy Awards
given to Walt Disney

132,549,000
visitors to Walt Disney
attractions in 2013

54
full-length animated
movies made by
Walt Disney Animation
Studios through 2014

around
78 million
Mickey Mouse ears sold
at Disneyland between
opening day and 2005

Walt Disney

Walter Elias "Walt" Disney was born on December 5, 1901, in Chicago, Illinois. From a young age, Walt loved to draw. He drew cartoons for his high school newspaper. He also took classes at the Chicago Academy of Fine Arts. In 1919, Walt moved to Kansas City, Missouri. There, he was hired to draw cartoons for **advertisements**. This job did not last long, but soon he had another that was even better. He drew moving cartoon ads for a film advertisement company. Walt started learning all he could about **animated** cartoons.

In 1922, Walt quit his job to focus on his own company. He had started a cartoon company called Laugh-O-Gram Films with a friend. They created funny cartoon characters. The business was not successful, but Walt did not give up. A year later, he moved to Los Angeles, California. There, he started the Disney Brothers Studio with his brother, Roy.

Walter Elias Disney

7

The Birth of a Company

In 1926, Walt and Roy changed the name of their company to the Walt Disney Studio. The company struggled to find success. Then in 1927, the brothers created a cartoon character named Oswald the Lucky Rabbit. He was a hit in theaters. But despite Oswald's success, the company continued to face hard times. Again, Walt was not ready to give up. He was riding on a train when he began to draw a character similar to Oswald. The new character was a mouse with large, round ears. Walt named him Mickey Mouse.

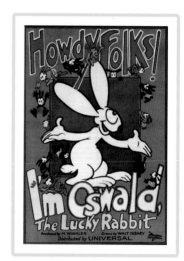

Mortimer or Mickey?

Mickey Mouse's original name was Mortimer Mouse. Walt Disney's wife, Lillian, did not like this name. She convinced her husband to change it to Mickey.

STEAMBOAT WILLIE

In November 1928, the Walt Disney Studio released its first Mickey Mouse cartoon. It was called *Steamboat Willie*. This was also the world's first cartoon with sound. The film was a huge sensation. It made Mickey Mouse famous. He became Disney's **mascot**. New characters soon followed. Pluto, Goofy, Donald Duck, and other Disney friends became stars!

In 1929, the studio was renamed Walt Disney Productions. In 1932, it made a cartoon called *Flowers and Trees*. This was the first cartoon made in full color. Walt's next goal was to make a longer movie. In 1934, the studio began work on *Snow White and the Seven Dwarfs*. Three years later, the film opened at a theater in Los Angeles. This was the world's first full-length animated movie. It was a huge success.

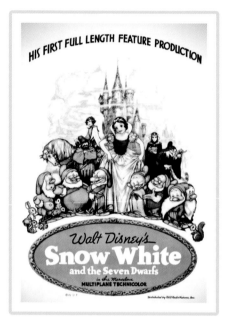

Walt and Roy used movie earnings to build a larger studio in Burbank, California. During the 1940s and 1950s, the studio made more full-length animated movies. Some, such as *Fantasia*, *Cinderella*, and *Peter Pan*, became classics. During this time, Disney also started making **live-action** movies. The first was called *Treasure Island*. It was an exciting tale about pirates. Disney also began making television shows such as *The Mickey Mouse Club*. Both film and television productions were hits.

Cinderella

Entertaining Families

Walt had more ideas. He decided to build a beautiful theme park called Disneyland in California. It would be a place for families to have fun together. In 1955, Disneyland opened its gates. Entrance cost only $1. The park included 5 themed lands and 18 **attractions**. At the center was Sleeping Beauty's castle. Children were thrilled to meet their favorite Disney characters. In less than two months, Disneyland had one million visitors.

Magic at Sea

Many families enjoy vacations at sea on the Disney Cruise Line. A popular stop is Castaway Cay, Disney's private island in the Bahamas. Here, cruisers swim, snorkel, and relax on the beach.

Walt Disney World

Walt began to plan a second theme park in Florida. Sadly, he died before it was built. However, Roy believed in his brother's dream. He took over construction of the park. In 1971, Walt Disney World opened in Orlando. It had many of the same attractions as Disneyland. But it was larger and better suited for crowds. It became more popular than the original. Today, Disneyland and Walt Disney World attract millions of visitors each year. People can also visit Disney parks in France, Hong Kong, Japan, and soon, China.

In 1986, the company was renamed The Walt Disney Company. Around this time, the company decided to focus on animated films again. The results were outstanding. Audiences loved *The Little Mermaid, Beauty and the Beast*, and *Aladdin*. Disney movies began to draw more crowds than ever. *The Lion King* broke **box office** records. Disney also began to work with Pixar Animation Studios to create films with **CGI animation**. Together, they produced favorites such as *Finding Nemo* and *Toy Story*.

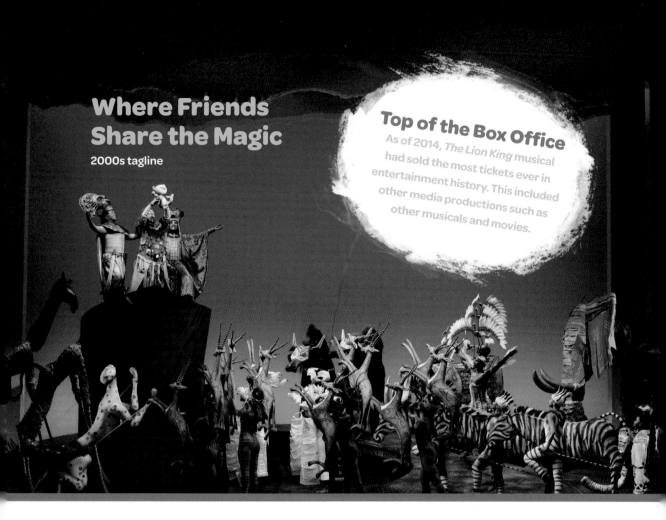

Where Friends Share the Magic

2000s tagline

Top of the Box Office

As of 2014, *The Lion King* musical had sold the most tickets ever in entertainment history. This included other media productions such as other musicals and movies.

Disney soon turned its success in films to live shows. Popular movies such as *Beauty and the Beast* and *The Lion King* were made into Broadway musicals. Famous characters come to life in these colorful productions. In *Disney on Ice*, figure skaters dress as Disney characters. They perform scenes from a variety of favorite Disney movies. *Disney Live* is for younger audiences. They enjoy watching Disney characters sing and dance on stage.

The Walt Disney Company has now expanded to include other companies. The company owns several television **networks**, including ABC and ESPN. One of its most popular networks is Disney Channel. This network offers programs for kids of all ages. It also airs original movies. Many young stars such as Selena Gomez and the Jonas Brothers have achieved worldwide fame after Disney Channel success.

Jonas Brothers

Disney also owns movie companies. In 2006, it bought Pixar Animation Studios. The team continues to make popular movies. *Cars*, *Up*, and *Toy Story 3* drew large audiences. Disney also owns Marvel Studios, famous for *Spider-Man* and other superhero movies. Most recently, Lucasfilm became a part of the Disney family. *Star Wars* fans look forward to Disney's release of the next movie in the series. Disney still makes its own movies as well. *Tangled* and *Frozen* saw great success. *Frozen* even won an **Academy Award** for Best Animated Feature Film. Disney continues to make magic through its many projects.

A History of Disney Animated Movies

1937	Snow White and the Seven Dwarfs
1940	Pinocchio
1942	Bambi
1950	Cinderella
1953	Peter Pan
1959	Sleeping Beauty
1961	101 Dalmatians
1967	The Jungle Book
1981	The Fox and the Hound
1989	The Little Mermaid
1991	Beauty and the Beast
1992	Aladdin
1994	The Lion King
1995	Pocahontas
1997	Hercules
1998	Mulan
1999	Tarzan
2008	Bolt
2009	The Princess and the Frog
2010	Tangled
2013	Frozen

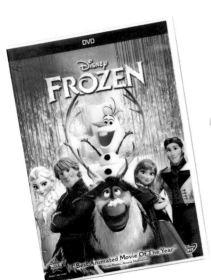

A Snowy Wonderland

Frozen is one of the most successful movies of all time. Ticket sales topped more than $1 billion.

Making Earth a Better Place

The Walt Disney Company also cares about the earth. Its **conservation** projects help protect habitats around the world. Many Disney projects protect **endangered** animals. These include loggerhead sea turtles, cotton-top tamarins, and western lowland gorillas. Some of these animals live on Disney properties. However, Disney also saves the lives of sick and injured animals around the world.

In 2008, The Walt Disney Studios started a film company called Disneynature. It makes movies about wildlife and nature. *Earth, Oceans*, and *Chimpanzee* are three box office hits. These movies raise money for causes as well as help people learn about nature. Ticket sales go to protect the subject of each film. *Earth* funded tree planting in Brazil, and *Oceans* helped with coral reef **restoration** in the Bahamas.

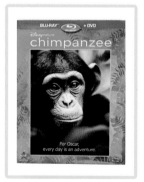

Money from *Chimpanzee* protects wild chimpanzees in Africa. Through these projects, Disney helps to make a better future for all living things.

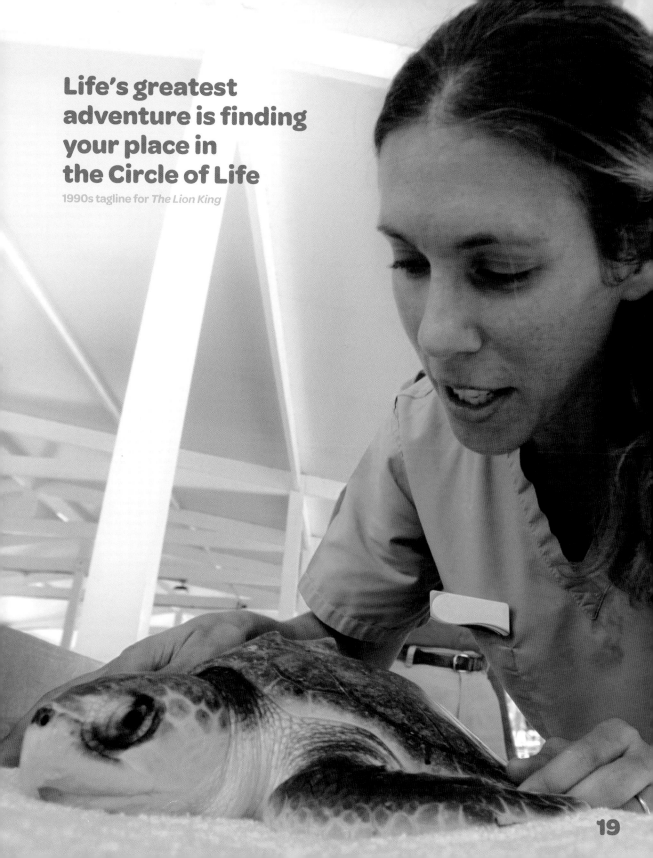

Life's greatest adventure is finding your place in the Circle of Life

1990s tagline for *The Lion King*

19

Disney Timeline

1901
Walter Elias Disney is
born in Chicago, Illinois,
on December 5

1926
The studio is
renamed the
Walt Disney Studio

1955
The Mickey Mouse Club
debuts on television

1950
Disney releases
Treasure Island, its
first live-action film

1932
Disney releases
Flowers and Trees, the
first full-color cartoon

1928
Steamboat Willie
opens in New York

1923
Walt and Roy Disney
open the Disney
Brothers Studio in
Los Angeles, California

1955
Disneyland opens in
Anaheim, California

1937
*Snow White and the
Seven Dwarfs* opens in
Los Angeles

1971
Walt Disney World opens
in Orlando, Florida

Disney · PIXAR

2006
Disney buys
Pixar Animation Studios

1992
Euro Disney Resort,
later renamed
Disneyland Paris,
opens in France

1994
Beauty and the Beast
opens on Broadway

1986
Company name changes to
The Walt Disney Company

2014
Frozen wins the
Academy Award for
Best Animated Feature

1966
Walt Disney
passes away on
December 15

Glossary

Academy Award—a yearly award presented for achievement in film; an Academy Award is also called an Oscar.

advertisements—notices and messages that announce or promote something

animated—produced by the creation of a series of drawings that are shown quickly, one after the other, to give the appearance of movement

attractions—things or places that draw visitors

box office—a measure of ticket sales sold by a film or other performance

brand—a category of products all made by the same company

CGI animation—artwork created by computers; CGI stands for computer-generated imagery.

conservation—the protection of animals, plants, and natural resources

endangered—at risk of becoming extinct

headquarters—a company's main office

live-action—films that are not made by animation; live-action movies feature human actors.

mascot—an animal or object used as a symbol by a group or company

networks—television companies that produce programs that people watch

reputable—respected and trusted by most people

restoration—to bring something back to its original state

To Learn More

AT THE LIBRARY

Bodden, Valerie. *The Story of Disney*. Mankato, Minn.: Creative Education, 2009.

Orr, Tamra B. *Walt Disney: The Man Behind the Magic*. New York, N.Y.: Children's Press, 2014.

Schroeder, Russell K. *Disney: The Ultimate Visual Guide*. New York, N.Y.: Dorling Kindersley, 2002.

ON THE WEB

Learning more about Disney is as easy as 1, 2, 3.

1. Go to www.factsurfer.com.

2. Enter "Disney" into the search box.

3. Click the "Surf" button and you will see a list of related web sites.

With factsurfer.com, finding more information is just a click away.

Index